·SEA AND COAST·

COLIN BAXTER

RICHARD DREW PUBLISHING
GLASGOW

Overleaf:
Isle of Lismore

WIDE CONTRASTS IN THE SCENERY OF SCOTLAND ALWAYS IMPRESS THE VISITOR. WHERE ELSE CAN BE FOUND IN SO SMALL AN AREA MOUNTAINS, SAVAGE SEAS, ROUGH COASTS, WOODED VALLEYS, WILD MOORLAND, TUMBLING RIVERS AND FERTILE PLAINS? CHANGING PLAY OF LIGHT BROUGHT BY THE FICKLE CLIMATE ADDS MYSTERY TO THE SCOTTISH EXPERIENCE.

NO-ONE IN RECENT YEARS HAS CAPTURED THIS EVER-CHANGING VARIETY AS SENSITIVELY AS THE PHOTOGRAPHER, COLIN BAXTER, WHO HAS IN THIS SERIES SELECTED CERTAIN AREAS AND THEMES TO CONVEY THE RICH DIVERSITY OF SCOTLAND'S CITIES AND COUNTRYSIDE.

SCOTLAND'S COASTLINE IS ONE OF THE LONGEST IN THE WORLD IN RELATION TO THE LAND MASS, FROM THE TWISTING, FJORD-LIKE SEA LOCHS OF THE WEST TO THE SEA CLIFFS AND MORE ROUNDED HEADLANDS OF THE EAST. AND EVERYWHERE BEAUTIFUL BEACHES, SOME OF SILVER SAND, AND MANY OF THEM LARGELY DESERTED. MOST STRIKING PERHAPS IS THE PROXIMITY OF SEA AND MOUNTAIN BOTH ON THE MAINLAND AND ON MANY OF THE WESTERN ISLES.

LAMLASH, ISLE OF ARRAN

UPPER
LOCH TORRIDON
AND LIATHACH

SUMMER ISLES,
WESTER ROSS

THE CUILLINS
AND LOCH SCAVAIG

LOCH SHIELDAIG,
TORRIDON

ULLAPOOL,
WESTER ROSS

THE NORTH SEA

MILLSTONE POINT,
BUTE

OVERLEAF:
LOCH TORRIDON,
WESTER ROSS

SCALPAY AND SKYE
FROM WESTER ROSS

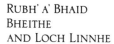

RUBH' A' BHAID
BHEITHE
AND LOCH LINNHE

GAIRLOCH,
WESTER ROSS

SCARBA
WITH MULL
IN THE DISTANCE

SHIELDAIG,
WESTER ROSS

EILEAN DONAN
CASTLE,
WESTER ROSS

ARDBAN AND RAASAY

FACING PAGE:
INNER SOUND
AND RAASAY

CROWLIN ISLANDS
FROM NEAR
CAMUSTEEL,
WESTER ROSS

REDPOINT,
WESTER ROSS

SGEIR GHLAS,
WESTER ROSS

Isle of Rona
from Wester Ross

Sunset

APPLECROSS,
WESTER ROSS
AND THE
ISLE OF RAASAY

LOCH LINNHE,
LORN

ANNAT BAY, LOCH BROOM,
WESTER ROSS

FIRTH OF FORTH

EAST COAST

FIRTH OF CLYDE

LOCH DIABAIG,
WESTER ROSS

BASS ROCK,
FIRTH OF FORTH

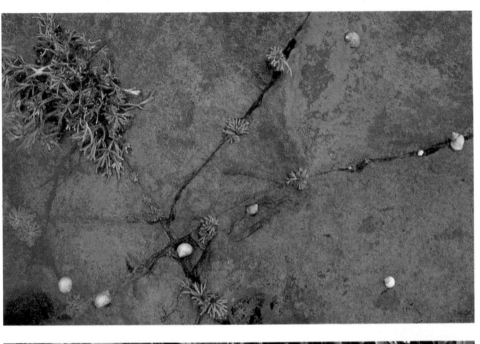

St Abb's Head,
Berwickshire

ARRAN
AND THE
FIRTH OF CLYDE

ARDNAMURCHAN

ISLES OF SCARBA
AND JURA

First Published 1986 by
RICHARD DREW PUBLISHING
6 CLAIRMONT GARDENS, GLASGOW, G3 7LW, SCOTLAND

Printed and bound in Great Britain by
Blantyre Printing and Binding Co. Ltd.

British Library Cataloguing in Publication Data

"Sea and coast — (Experience Scotland)
1. Coasts — Scotland — Guide-books
2. Scotland — Description and travel —
1981- — Guide-books
I. Title   II. Series
914.11'04858   DA870

ISBN 0-86267-157-4